Compiled by Ruth Cullen

PETER PAUPER PRESS, INC.
white plains, new york

Designed by Taryn Sefecka

Peter Pauper Press, Inc.
202 Mamaroneck Avenue
White Plains, NY 10601

ISBN 0-88088-292-1
Printed in China
7 6 5 4 3 2

Visit us at www.peterpauper.com

Seize
the
moment

INTRODUCTION

Get action.
Seize the moment.
Man was never
intended to
become an oyster.

THEODORE ROOSEVELT

Have you been putting off doing what you know you want to do? Are your own excuses tarting to wear you down? **Well, it's time to top thinking and start acting!**

Let the words in this book serve as your nspiration to do what you need to do—starting today. **Discover** a new rallying cry and hout it from the rooftops. Find the motivaion to take that first step, no matter how mall. And know that today is a gift, filled with opportunity, beauty, and joy.

R. C.

Take a chance!
All life is a chance.
The man who goes the
furthest is generally
the one who is willing
to do and dare.

DALE CARNEGIE

Love the moment,
and the energy
of that moment
will spread beyond
all boundaries.

CORITA KENT

Don't wait for
extraordinary opportunities.
Seize common occasions
and make them great.

ORISON SWETT MARDEN

What would it be like if you
lived each day, each breath,
as a work of art in progress?
Imagine that you are a
Masterpiece unfolding,
every second of every day,
a work of art taking form
with every breath.

THOMAS CRUM

Awaken your sense, your
intuition, your desires.
Awaken the parts of yourself
that have been sleeping.
Life is a dream, and to live it,
you must be awake.

RACHEL SNYDER

If you surrender completely to the moments as they pass, you live more richly those moments.

ANNE MORROW LINDBERGH

Let us wipe out the past, trust in the future, and rejoice in the glorious Now.

WILLIAM R. EVANS III &
ANDREW FROTHINGHAM

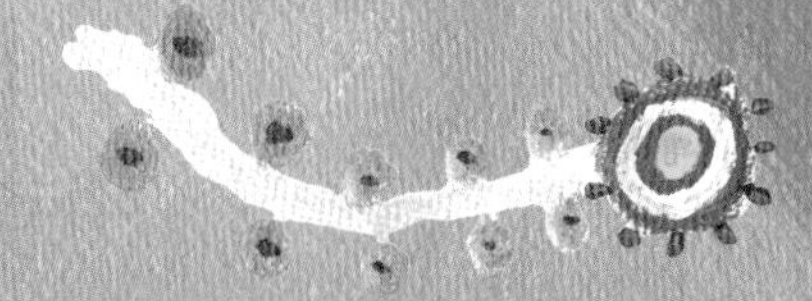

DO IT NOW!

Today will be yesterday tomorrow.

E. C. MCKENZIE

Dost thou love life? Then do not squander time, for time is the stuff life is made of.

BENJAMIN FRANKLIN

Gather ye rosebuds
while ye may,
Old Time is still a-flying:
And this same flower
that smiles today
Tomorrow will be dying.

ROBERT HERRICK

To live exhilaratingly
in and for the moment
is deadly serious work,
fun of the most
exhausting sort.

BARBARA GRIZZUTI HARRISON

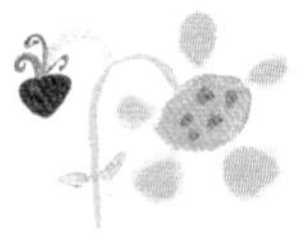

Seize today,
and put as
little trust
as you can
in tomorrow.

HORACE

Whatever you can do,
or dream you can, begin it.
Boldness has genius,
power, and magic in it.

JOHANN WOLFGANG
VON GOETHE

My philosophy is that
not only are you responsible
for your life, but doing
the best at this moment
puts you in the best place
for the next moment.

OPRAH WINFREY

Trust no Future, howe'er pleasant!
Let the dead Past bury its dead:
Act,—act in the living Present!
Heart within, and God o'erhead!

HENRY WADSWORTH LONGFELLOW

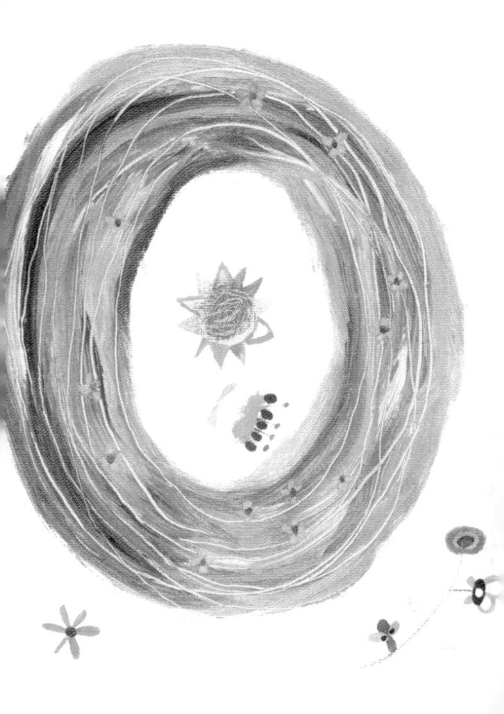

Live your life each day as
you would climb a mountain. . .
Climb slowly, steadily,
enjoying each passing moment;
and the view from the
summit will serve as a
fitting climax for
the journey.

HAROLD V. MELCHERT

I recommend you
to take care of
the minutes:
for hours will
take care
of themselves.

LORD CHESTERFIELD

Time **was** is past—
thou canst it not recall.
Time **is** thou hast—
employ thy portion small.
Time **future** is not, and
may never be. Time **present**
is the only time for thee!

INSCRIPTION ON
AN ANCIENT SUN DIAL

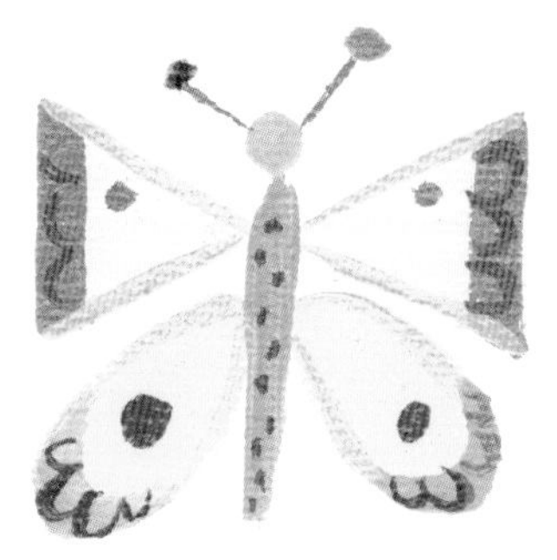

We must use time
as a tool,
not as a couch.

JOHN F. KENNEDY

To change one's life,
start immediately,
do it flamboyantly,
no exceptions.

WILLIAM JAMES

Hoist up sail
while gale doth last,
Tide and wind stay
no man's pleasure.

ROBERT SOUTHWELL

Preach! Write! Act!
Do any thing,
save to lie down
and die!

NATHANIEL HAWTHORNE

He that will not
when he may,
When he will
he shall have nay.

ROBERT BURTON

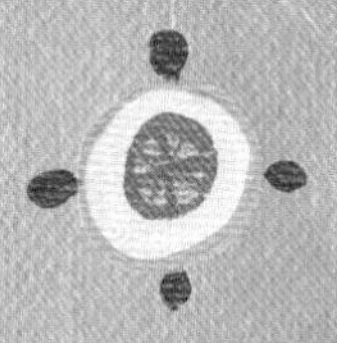

Do what you can,
with what you have,
where you are.

THEODORE ROOSEVELT

Well done
is better than
well said.

BENJAMIN FRANKLIN

Whatever your next
challenge may be, do it well!
Do it with tolerance and
understanding of others.
But, do it with all of the
drive, enthusiasm and
joy of life you have in you.

DONALD RUMSFELD

Only as I am aware
of the present will I
have the opportunity
to be fully alive.

ANNE WILSON SCHAEF

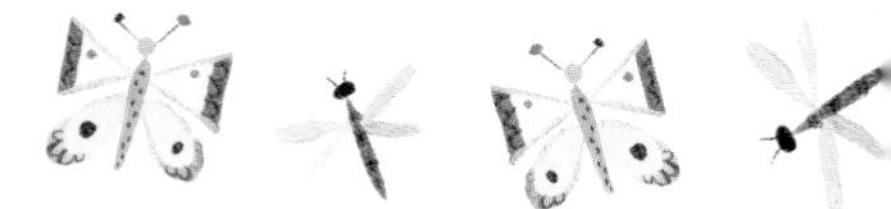

Every new day
begins with possibilities.
It's up to us to fill it with
the things that move us
toward progress and peace.

RONALD REAGAN

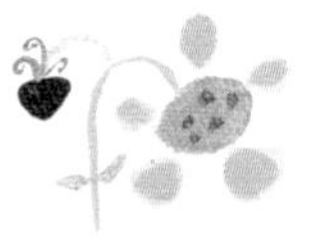

The people who get on
in this world are the people
who get up and look for the
circumstances they want, and,
if they can't find them,
make them.

GEORGE BERNARD SHAW

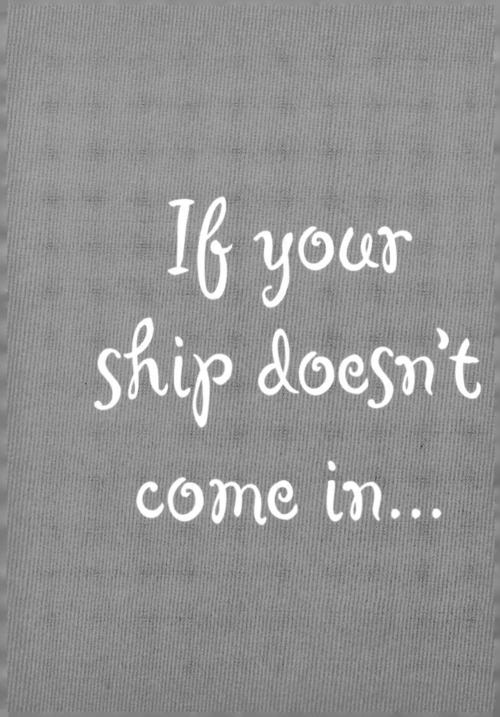
If your
ship doesn't
come in...

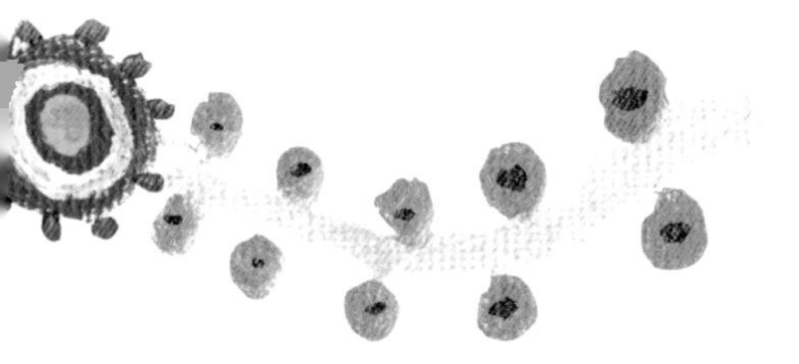

..swim out to it!

JONATHAN WINTERS

Whether you believe you can do a thing or not, you're right.

ATTRIBUTED TO HENRY FORD

If you risk
nothing,
then you risk
everything.

GEENA DAVIS

Don't worry about the future,
The present is all thou hast,
The future will soon be present,
And the present will soon be past.

WILLIAM R. EVANS III &
ANDREW FROTHINGHAM

The minute you
settle for less than
you deserve, you get
even less than
you settled for.

MAUREEN DOWD

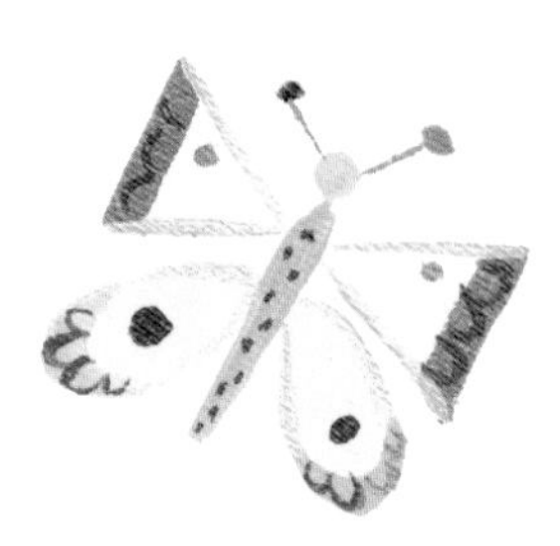

It's all right to have butterflies in your stomach. Just get them to fly in formation.

DR. ROB GILBERT

The only thing that will stop you from fulfilling your dreams is you.

TOM BRADLEY

One can
never consent
to creep when
one feels
an impulse

HELEN KELLER

Opportunities don't knock at all. They don't have to, they're already all around us. It's up to us to see where they are and take advantage of them.

DAVE THOMAS

The greatest
mistake you can make
in life is continually
to be fearing
you will make one.

ELBERT HUBBARD

What would you do if you weren't afraid?

SPENCER JOHNSON

What you
will do matters.
All you need is
to do it.

JUDY GRAHN

To be a great champion you must believe you are the best. If you're not, pretend you are.

MUHAMMAD ALI

Nobody got anywhere in this world by simply being content.

LOUIS L'AMOUR

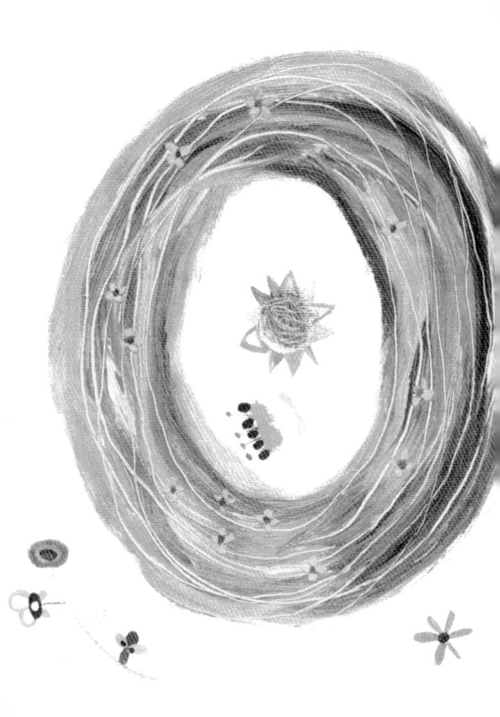

Hitch your wagon to a star.

RALPH WALDO EMERSON

A life spent making mistakes is not only more honorable, but more useful than a life spent doing nothing.

GEORGE BERNARD SHAW

If one advances
confidently in the
direction of his dreams . . .
he will meet with a
success unexpected in
common hours.

HENRY DAVID THOREAU

It's not whether you get
knocked down;
it's whether you get up.

VINCE LOMBARDI

They always say that
time changes things,
but you actually have
to change them yourself.

ANDY WARHOL

Many people are so afraid to die that they never begin to live.

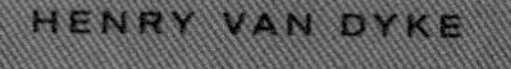

Just don't give up trying to do what you really want to do. Where there's love and inspiration, I don't think you can go wrong.

ELLA FITZGERALD

What a wonderful
life I've had!
I only wish I'd
realized it sooner.

COLETTE

It is better to die
on your feet than to
live on your knees.

DOLORES IBARRURI

Live for today;
plan for tomorrow;
remember yesterday.

AESOP

Don't be afraid your
life will end, be afraid that
it will never begin.

GRACE HANSEN

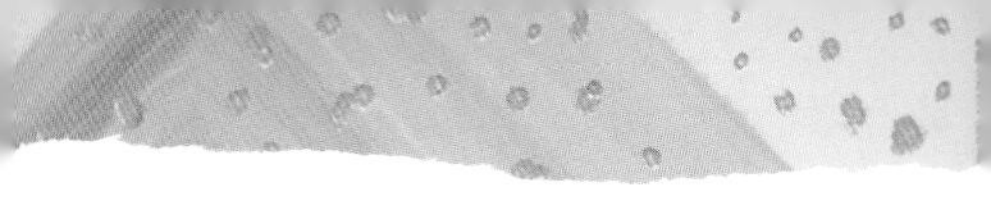

There are two things
to aim at in life:
first, to get what you want;
and, after that, to enjoy it.
Only the wisest of mankind
achieve the second.

LOGAN PEARSALL SMITH

Do all the good you can,
By all the means you can,
In all the ways you can,
In all the places you can,
At all the times you can,
To all the people you can,
As long as ever you can.

JOHN WESLEY

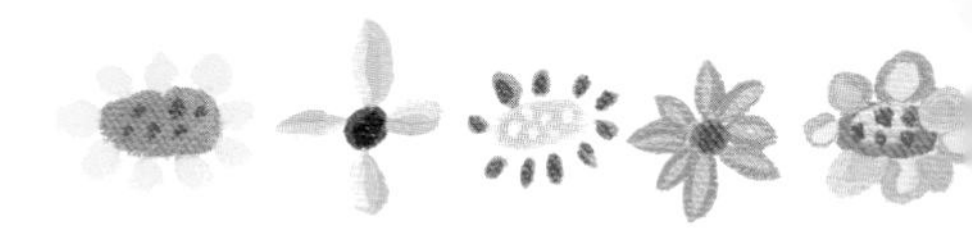

Every day,
I wish to make the
world more beautiful
than I found it.

MADAME DE POMPADOUR

Light tomorrow with today!

ELIZABETH BARRETT BROWNING

May you live...

. . . all the days
of your life.

JONATHAN SWIFT

I do not intend to pause, or rest, or rust.

DR. GEORGE SHEEHAN,
60-YEAR-OLD MARATHONER

Find the joy in life,
because as Ferris Bueller
said on his day off,
"Life moves pretty fast and
if you don't stop and look
around once in a while,
you are going to miss it."

BARBARA BUSH

You don't get to choose how you're going to die. Or when. You can only decide how you're going to live. Now.

JOAN BAEZ

My deepest belief
is that living as if
you are dying
sets us free.

ANNE LAMOTT

Learning to live in the present tense—one that's free from the failures of the past and the anxieties of the future—is a wonderful gift, and one you always should be striving for.

RICK PITINO

While life lasts, it's good to
remember that death is coming,
and it's good that we don't
know when. It keeps us alert.
It reminds us to live while we have
the chance. Somebody should tell
us that we are dying. Then we
might live life to the limit,
every minute of every day.

MICHAEL LANDON

You will never experience the earth with all its wonders in this time again. Don't wait for one

last look at the ocean,
the sky, the stars,
or a loved one.
Go look now.

ELISABETH KÜBLER-ROSS AND
DAVID KESSLER

At every age, you have the
opportunity to star in your
own adventure. . . .
The story of your life is
about one thing only—you.
What you make of it . . .
will be the tale that's written.
It's your choice how the story ends.

JUDGE JUDY SHEINDLIN